THE FUNNIEST QUOTES BOOK
1001 OF THE BEST HUMOROUS QUOTATIONS

BY M. PREFONTAINE

Published by MP Publishing
Copyright © 2016

OTHER BOOKS BY THE AUTHOR INCLUDE

The Big Book of Quotes

The Book of Best Sports Quotes

The Book of Funny Sports Quotes

501 Quotes about Life

501 Quotes about Love

An Inspirational Quote a Day

Quotes: The Box Set

CONTENTS

INTRODUCTION

A fine quotation is a diamond in the hand of a man of wit and a pebble in the hand of a fool.
Joseph Roux

This is a collection of the funniest quotes culled by the author from the thousands that are out there to save the reader the trouble of perusing the multitude of mediocre to find the best. This is a book which you can just pick up anytime and carry on where you left off last time. It is for those who want to pep up a speech, a presentation or an email and for those who just want to sit at home and enjoy the best humorous quotations for their own amusement.

In the author's view the best humorous quotations are often those which contain an essence of truth viewed from an unexpected and quirky angle unseen previously.

This collection is a miscellany from many individuals and are ordered into forty broad subject areas. I hope you will find many diamonds to amuse you.

M. Prefontaine

CHAPTER 1: ALCOHOL

A bartender is just a pharmacist with a limited inventory.
Anon

Beer is living proof that God loves us and wants us to be happy.
Benjamin Franklin

I'm not as think as you drunk I am.
Mega Jones

There are better things in life than alcohol, but alcohol makes up for not having them.
Terry Pratchett

Beauty is in the eye of the beer holder.
Anon

There's nothing wrong with sobriety in moderation.
John Ciardi

Abstainer: a weak person who yields to the temptation of denying himself a pleasure.
Ambrose Bierce

Work is the curse of the drinking classes.
Oscar Wilde

You can't be a real country unless you have a beer and an airline - it helps if you have some kind of football team, or some nuclear weapons, but in the very least you need a beer.
Frank Zappa

I'd tried to straighten him out, but there's only so much you can do for a person who thinks Auschwitz is a brand of beer.
David Sedaris

Everybody has to believe in something.... I believe I'll have another drink.
W.C. Fields

The problem with Marxism is the proletariat isn't going to rise up against capitalism and consumerism. The only time they'll rise up is during a commercial break to either go to the bathroom or grab more beer.
Jarod Kintz

Beer is the reason I get out of bed every afternoon.
Anon

Drinking beer doesn't make you fat, it makes you lean.... against bars, tables, chairs, and poles.
Gerard Way

A drunk man's words are a sober man's thoughts.
Steve Fergosi

Whoever drinks beer, he is quick to sleep; whoever sleeps long, does not sin; whoever does not sin, enters Heaven! Thus, let us drink beer!
Martin Luther

There are more old drunks than there are old doctors.
Willie Nelson

Pain makes you stronger. Tears make you braver. Heartbreak makes you wiser. And vodka makes you not remember any of that crap.
Nishan Panwar

I went out with a guy who once told me I didn't need to drink to make myself more fun to be around. I told him, I'm drinking so that you're more fun to be around.
Chelsea Handler

Ah, beer. The cause of and the solution to all of life's problems.
Homer Simpson

An alcoholic is someone you don't like who drinks just as much as you do.
Dylan Thomas

You're not drunk if you can lie on the floor without holding on.
Dean Martin

I like to have a martini,
Two at the very most.
After three I'm under the table,
After four I'm under my host.
Dorothy Parker

One tequila, two tequila, three tequila, floor.
Buddy Shirt

Between the revolution and the firing squad there is always time for a bottle of champagne.
Prince Boris Mizorzky

Beer makes you smarter. It made bud wiser.
Bill Mather

I have taken more out of alcohol than alcohol has taken out of me.
Winston Churchill

In 1969 I gave up women and alcohol. It was he worst twenty minute of my life.
George Best

I am not a heavy drinker. Sometimes I can go hours without a drink.
Noel Coward

99% of all problems can be solved by money -- and for the other 1% there's alcohol.
Quentin R. Bufogle

Hangover: The wrath of grapes.
Dorothy Parker

American beer is served cold so you can tell it from urine.
David Moulton

The hard thing about being a bartender is figuring out who is drunk and who is just stupid.
Richard Braunstein

I'm going to be around until the Atomic Energy Commission finds a safe place to bury my liver.
Phil Harris

Wine is sunlight, held together by water.
Galileo

I was one drink away from a tattoo.
Lily Savage

It is kind of ironic that they caution pregnant women not to drink alcohol in case it harms the baby. If it wasn't for alcohol most women wouldn't be that way.

Rita Rudner

Those who drink to drown their sorrows should be told that sorrows know how to swim.

Ann Landers

CHAPTER 2: BUSINESS

A bargain is something you don't need at a price you can't resist.
Franklin Jones

Opportunities come infrequently. When it rains gold, put out the bucket, not the thimble.
Warren Buffet

The key to being a good manager is keeping the people who hate you away from those who are still undecided.
Casey Stengel

By working faithfully eight hours a day you may eventually get to be boss and work twelve hours a day.
Robert Frost

The quickest way to make a million? Marry it.
Zsa Zsa Gabor

If I had asked people what they wanted, they would have said faster horses.
Henry Ford

To err is human, to blame it on somebody else shows management potential.
Anon

When people ask me how many people work here, I say, about a third of them –
Lisa Kennedy Montgomery

When opportunity knocks, some people are in the backyard looking for four-leaf clovers.
Polish Proverb

I always arrive late at the office, but I make up for it by leaving early.
Charles Lamb

Take all the fools out of this world and there wouldn't be any fun living in it, or profit.
Josh Billings

I don't want yes-men around me. I want everyone to tell the truth, even if it costs them their jobs.
Samuel Goldwyn

Nobody ever went broke underestimating the taste of the American public.
HL Mencken

There is nothing more essential to getting a project off the ground than the underestimate.
Robert Brault

Business is the art of extracting money from another man's pocket without resorting to violence.
Max Amsterdam

I always invest in companies that an idiot could run because one day they will.
Warren Buffet

The very first law in advertising is to avoid the concrete promise and cultivate the delightfully vague.
Bill Cosby

We have long felt that the only value of stock forecasters is to make fortune-tellers look good.
Warren Buffett

If you see a bandwagon, it's too late.
James Goldsmith

Ability is what will get you to the top if the boss has no daughter.
Anon

Early to bed and early to rise probably indicates unskilled labor.
John Ciardi

Every employee rises to the level of his own incompetence.
Laurence J. Peter -The Peter Principle

Indecision is the key to flexibility.
Anon

Luck is what happens when preparation meets opportunity.
Seneca

Too bad all the people who know how to run the country are busy driving taxis and cutting hair.
George Burns

Not doing more than the average is what keeps the average down.
William Lyon Phelps

Some people make things happen, some watch things happen, while others wonder what has happened.
Proverb

Expect the best. Prepare for the worst. Capitalize on what comes.
Zig Ziglar

Formal education will make you a living. Self-education will make you a fortune.
Jim Rohn

Rule No.1: Never lose money. Rule No.2: Never forget rule No.1.
Warren Buffett

Only when the tide goes out do you discover who's been swimming naked.
Warren Buffett

If you've been playing poker for half an hour and you still don't know who the patsy is, you're the patsy.
Warren Buffett

What the wise do in the beginning, fools do in the end.
Warren Buffett

Kill my boss? Do I dare live out the American dream?
Homer Simpson

Why is it that when my alarm goes off at 6 am and I close my eyes for 5 minutes, it's suddenly 7:30. And when it's 1:30 pm at the office and I close my eyes for 5 minutes, it's only 1:31?
Garry Shandling

A lot of people become pessimists from financing optimists.
Anon

Art is making something out of nothing and selling it.
Frank Zappa

CHAPTER 3: CHILDREN

I told my wife I don't want to be there at the birth. I don't see why my evening should be ruined too.
Dennis Wolfburg

A baby is nothing more than a loud noise at one end and no sense of responsibility at the other.
Ronald Knox

Experts say you should never hit your children in anger. When is a good time? When you're feeling festive?
Roseanne Barr

Adults are just obsolete children.
Dr. Seuss

The trouble with children is that they are not returnable.
Quentin Crisp

To lose one parent may be regarded as a misfortune; to lose both looks like carelessness.
Oscar Wilde

A baby is God's opinion that the world should go on.
Carl Sandburg

Children are the living messages we send to a time we will not see.
John W. Whitehead

In America there are two classes of travel – first class, and with children.
Robert Benchley

The easiest way to teach children the value of money is to borrow some from them.
Anon

Like fruit, children are sweetest just before they turn bad.
Dena Groquet

Insanity is hereditary: You can get it from your children.
Sam Levinson

Raising kids is part joy and part guerilla warfare.
Ed Asner

Having one child makes you a parent; having two you are a referee.
David Frost

If you have never been hated by your child, you have never been a parent.
Bette Davis

Children begin by loving their parents; as they grow older they judge them; sometimes they forgive them.
Oscar Wilde

Times are bad. Children no longer obey their parents, and everyone is writing a book.
Marcus Tullius Cicero

Don't worry that children never listen to you; worry that they are always watching you.
Robert Fulghum

A characteristic of the normal child is he doesn't act that way very often.
Anon

Cleaning your house while your kids are still growing up is like shoveling the walk before it stops snowing.
Phylliss Diller

Children find everything in nothing; men find nothing in everything.
Giacomo Leopardi

A three-year-old child is a being who gets almost as much fun out of a fifty-six dollar set of swings as it does out of finding a small green worm.
Bill Vaughan

As the father of two young girls, I have come to the realization that they are just as messy as boys but the dirt that they create around the house is comprised of at least 50% glitter.
Andrew K. Keller

There are only two things a child will share willingly — communicable diseases and his mother's age.
Benjamin Spock

Having a two-year-old is like having a blender that you don't have the top for.
Jerry Seinfeld

It's a funny thing about mothers and fathers. Even when their own child is the most disgusting little blister you could ever imagine, they still think that he or she is wonderful.
Roald Dahl

I played with my grandfather a lot when I was a kid. He was dead, but my parents had him cremated and put his ashes in an Etch-a-Sketch.
Alan Harvey

I have found the best way to give advice to children is to find out what they want and then advise them to do it.
Harry S Truman

Never raise your hand to your children – it leaves your mid-section unprotected.
Robert Orben

If I ever had twins I would use one for parts.
Steven Wright

I'm in that benign form of house arrest that is looking after a baby.
JK Rowling

Oh what a tangled web we weave when first we practice to conceive.
Don Herold

By far the most common craving of pregnant women is not to be pregnant.
Phyllis Diller

I got married and we had a baby nine months and ten seconds later.
Jayne Mansfield

We never really grow up; we only learn how to act in public.
Bryan White

CHAPTER 4: DEATH

I'm not afraid of death; I just don't want to be there when it happens.
Woody Allen

Unbeing dead isn't being alive.
E.E. Cummings

When I die, I want to go peacefully like my grandfather did–in his sleep. Not yelling and screaming like the passengers in his car.
Bob Monkhouse

First the doctor told me the good news: I was going to have a disease named after me.
Steve Martin

All men are cremated equal.
Spike Milligan

I didn't attend the funeral, but I sent a nice letter saying I approved of it.
Mark Twain

I intend to live forever. So far, so good.
Steven Wright

According to most studies, people's number one fear is public speaking. Number two is death. Death is number two! Does that sound right? That means to the average person, if you go to a funeral, you're better off in the casket than doing the eulogy.
Jerry Seinfeld

The best cure for sea sickness is to sit under a tree.
Spike Milligan

You know you're getting old when you stoop to tie your shoelaces and wonder what else you could do while you're down there.
George Burns

Life expectancy would grow by leaps and bounds if green vegetables smelled as good as bacon.
Doug Larson

Never do anything that you wouldn't want to explain to the paramedics.
Anon

Life is a long agonized illness only curable by death.
Spike Milligan

The patient is not likely to recover who makes the doctor his heir.
Thomas Fuller

Always go to other people's funerals, otherwise they won't come to yours.
Yogi Berra

Don't worry about the world coming to an end today. It is already tomorrow in Australia.
Charles Schulz

Dying is a very dull, dreary affair. And my advice to you is to have nothing whatever to do with it.
Somerset Maughan

Immortality: a fate worse than death.
Edgar Shoaff

Once the game is over, the king and the pawn go back into the same box.
Italian Proverb

Die, my dear doctor! That's the last thing I shall do!
Lord Palmerston

Whenever I watch TV and see those poor starving kids all over the world, I can't help but cry. I mean I'd love to be skinny like that but not with all those flies and death and stuff.
Mariah Carey

I'd love to slit my mother-in-law's corsets and watch her spread to death.
Phyllis Diller

I'm very pleased to be here. Let's face it, at my age I'm very pleased to be anywhere.
George Burns

My grandmother was a very tough woman. She buried three husbands and two of them were just napping.
Rita Rudner.

When I came back to Dublin I was court-martialed in my absence and sentenced to death in my absence, so I said they could shoot me in my absence.
Brendan Behan

A thing is not necessarily true because a man dies for it.
Oscar Wilde

I do not fear death. I had been dead for billions and billions of years before I was born, and had not suffered the slightest inconvenience from it.
Mark Twain

One lives in the hope of becoming a memory.
Antonio Porchia

I'll tell you what makes my blood boil – crematoriums.
Tim Vine

I believe you should live each day as if it is your last, which is why I don't have any clean laundry, because, come on, who wants to wash clothes on the last day of their life?
Jack Handey

In heaven all the interesting people are missing.
Friedrich Wilhelm Nietzsche

I would never die for my beliefs because I might be wrong.
Bertrand Russell

I hope that after I die, people will say of me: "That guy sure owed me a lot of money."
Jack Handy

Death is nature's way of telling you to slow down.
Anon

CHAPTER 5: DEBT

Christmas is the season when you buy this year's gifts with next year's money.
Anon

Creditors have better memories than debtors.
Benjamin Franklin

If you think nobody cares if you're alive, try missing a couple of car payments.
Earl Wilson

Today, there are three kinds of people: the have's, the have-not's, and the have-not-paid-for-what-they-have's.
Earl Wilson

Blessed are the young, for they shall inherit the national debt.
Herbert Hoover

A billion here, a billion there, sooner or later it adds up to real money.
Everett Dirksen

Bankruptcy stared me in the face, but one thought kept me calm; soon I'd be too poor to need an anti-theft alarm.
Gina Rothfels

I'm living so far beyond my income that we may almost be said to be living apart.
E.E. Cummings

The ideas of debtor and creditor as to what constitutes a good time never coincide.
P.G. Wodehouse

It is said that the world is in a state of bankruptcy, that the world owes the world more than the world can pay.
Ralph Waldo Emerson

Debts are like children: the smaller they are the more noise they make.
Spanish Proverb

Running into debt isn't so bad. It's running into creditors that hurts.
Anon

I like my players to be married and in debt. That's the way you motivate them.
Ernie Banks

CHAPTER 6: EDUCATION

But there are advantages to being elected President. The day after I was elected, I had my high school grades classified Top Secret.
Ronald Reagan

I won't say ours was a tough school, but we had our own coroner. We used to write essays like: What I'm going to be if I grow up.
Lenny Bruce

I never let my schooling interfere with my education
Anon

It is a miracle that curiosity survives formal education.
Albert Einstein

My school days were the happiest days of my life; which should give you some indication of the misery I've endured over the past twenty-five years.
Paul Merton

Education is learning what you didn't even know you didn't know.
Daniel J. Boorstin

You may be a redneck if... you have spent more on your pickup truck than on your education.
Jeff Foxworthy

The only educational aspect of television is that it puts the repair man's kids through college.
Joan Welsh

I'm not going to buy my kids an encyclopedia. Let them walk to school like I did.
Yogi Berra

In the first place, God made idiots. That was for practice. Then he made school boards.
Mark Twain

I read in the newspapers they are going to have 30 minutes of intellectual stuff on television every Monday from 7:30 to 8. to educate America. They couldn't educate America if they started at 6:30.
Groucho Marx

Our bombs are smarter than the average high school student. At least they can find Kuwait.
A. Whitney Brown

Education is the inculcation of the incomprehensible into the ignorant by the incompetent.
Josiah Stamp

His lack of education is more than compensated for by his keenly developed moral bankruptcy.
Woody Allen

My act is very educational. I heard a man leaving the other night saying, 'Well that taught me a lesson'.
Ken Dodd

You know there is a problem with the education system when you realize that out of the 3 R's only one begins with an R.
Dennis Miller

Education is what remains after one has forgotten what one has learned in school.

John Dryden

Education: that which reveals to the wise, and conceals from the stupid, the vast limits of their knowledge.

Mark Twain

If you think education is expensive, try ignorance!

Andy McIntyre

A gentleman need not know Latin, but he should at least have forgotten it.

Brander Matthews

Colleges are places where pebbles are polished and diamonds are dimmed.

R.S. Ingersoll

The mark of a true MBA is that he is often wrong but seldom in doubt.

Robert Buzzell

A man who has never gone to school may steal from a freight car; but if he has a university education, he may steal the whole railroad.

Theodore Roosevelt

Ever wonder if illiterate people get the full effect of alphabet soup?

John Mendosa

Economists report that a college education adds many thousands of dollars to a man's lifetime income—which he then spends sending his son to college.

Bill Vaughn

A graduation ceremony is an event where the commencement speaker tells thousands of students dressed in identical caps and gowns that 'individuality' is the key to success.

Robert Orben

CHAPTER 7: FAMILY

By the time a man realizes that his father was right, he has a son who thinks he's wrong.
Charles Wadsworth

A baby is a loud noise at one end and no sense of responsibility at the other
Ronald Knox

Before I got married I had six theories about bringing up children; now I have six children and no theories.
John Wilmott

Some family trees bear an enormous crop of nuts.
Wayne H.

People who say they sleep like a baby usually don't have one
Leo J. Burke

If your family tree does not fork, you might be a redneck.
Jeff Foxworthy

Behind every successful man stands a surprised mother-in-law.
Hubert Humphrey

It is amazing how quickly the kids learn to drive a car, yet are unable to understand the lawn mower, snow blower and vacuum cleaner.
Ben Bergor

My husband wanted one of those big-screen TVs for his birthday. So I just moved his chair closer to the one we have already.

Wendy Liebman

Nature gives us twelve years to develop a love for our children before turning them into teenagers

William Galvin

Teenagers complain there's nothing to do, then stay out all night doing it

Bob Phillips

The best time to give advice to your children is while they're still young enough to believe you know what you're talking about.

Evan Esar

Middle Age: When you begin to exchange your emotions for symptoms

Georges Clemenceau

Middle age is having a choice between two temptations and choosing the one that'll get you home earlier

Dan Bennett

The really frightening thing about middle age is the knowledge that you'll grow out of it.

Doris Day

My Father had a profound influence on me. He was a lunatic.

Spike Milligan

My God. We've had cloning in the South for years. It's called cousins.
Robin Williams

For birth control I rely on my personality.
Milt Able

Familiarity breeds contempt and children.
Mark Twain

CHAPTER 8: FASHION

A lot of gay men stay in the closet because they are interested in fashion.
George Carlin

One is never over-dressed or underdressed with a Little Black Dress.
Karl Lagerfeld

You can never be overdressed or overeducated.
Oscar Wilde

Whoever said that money can't buy happiness, simply didn't know where to go shopping.
Bo Derek

Dress shabbily and they remember the dress; dress impeccably and they remember the woman.
Coco Chanel

I like my money right where I can see it: hanging in my closet.
Carrie Bradshaw

Some of the worst mistakes in my life were haircuts.
Jim Morrison

Style is when they're running you out of town and you make it look like you're leading the parade.
William Battie

Every generation laughs at the old fashions, but follows religiously the new.
Henry David Thoreau

Fashion is a form of ugliness so intolerable that we have to alter it every six months.
Oscar Wilde

If I want to knock a story off the front page, I just change my hairstyle.
Hillary Rodham Clinton

A woman's dress should be a like a barbed-wire fence: serving its purpose without obstructing the view.
Sophia Loren

It costs a lot of money to look this cheap.
Dolly Parton

So soon as a fashion is Universal, it is out of date.
Marie Von Ebner-Eschenbach

She wore far too much rouge last night and not quite enough clothes. That is always a sign of despair in a woman.
Oscar Wilde

She looked as if she had been poured into her clothes and had forgotten to say "when".
P. G. Wodehouse

Only men who are not interested in women are interested in women's clothes. Men who like women never notice what they wear.
Anatole France

Once you can accept the universe as matter expanding into nothing that is something, wearing stripes with plaid comes easy.
Anon

CHAPTER 9: FOOD

I read recipes the same way I read science fiction. I get to the end and I think, "Well, that's not going to happen".
Anon

The trouble with eating Italian food is that five or six days later, you're hungry again.
George Miller

Inside me there's a thin person struggling to get out, but I can usually sedate him with four or five cupcakes.
Bob Thaves

Avoid fruits and nuts. You are what you eat.
Jim Davis

Ham and eggs—a day's work for a chicken; a lifetime commitment for a pig.
Anon

I used to eat a lot of natural foods until I learned that most people die of natural causes.
Anon

Never eat more than you can lift.
Miss Piggy

Cucumber should be well sliced, dressed with pepper and vinegar, and then thrown out.
Samuel Johnson

The two biggest sellers in bookstores are the cookbooks and the diet books. The cookbooks tell you how to prepare the food and the diet books tell you how not to eat any of it.
Andy Rooney

In Mexico, we have a word for sushi: bait.
José Simons

When the waitress asked if I wanted my pizza cut into four or eight slices, I said, 'Four. I don't think I can eat eight.'
Yogi Berra

The most remarkable thing about my mother is that for 30 years she served the family nothing but leftovers. The original meal has never been found.
Calvin Trillin

Ask not what you can do for your country. Ask what's for lunch.
Orson Welles

I always cook with wine. Sometimes I even add it to the food.
W.C. Fields

Humor keeps us alive. Humor and food. Don't forget food. You can go a week without laughing.
Joss Whedon

Give a man a fish, and you'll feed him for a day. Teach a man to fish, and he'll buy a funny hat. Talk to a hungry man about fish, and he's a consultant.
Scott Adams

He was a bold man that first did eat an oyster.
Johnathan Swift

You are what what you eat eats.
Michael Pollan

The only way to keep your health is to eat what you don't want, drink what you don't like, and do what you'd rather not.
Mark Twain

The noblest of dogs is the hot dog, it feeds the hand that bites it.
Anon

CHAPTER 10: FRIENDSHIP

Friendship is like peeing on yourself: everyone can see it, but only you get the warm feeling that it brings.
Robert Bloch

Outside of a dog, a book is man's best friend. Inside of a dog it's too dark to read.
Groucho Marx

I notice my wife when she's on the phone with her friends, man they will share every intimate details of their lives with each other. See men once we become friends with another man we may never say another word to him, unless there's valuable information that needs to be exchanged. Things like 'Hey Jim, your shirt's on fire'.
Jeff Foxworthy

No one is completely unhappy at the failure of his best friend.
Groucho Marx

A good friend will help you move. But a best friend will help you move a dead body.
Jim Hayes

A true friend stabs you in the front.
Oscar Wilde

Lots of people want to ride with you in the limo, but what you want is someone who will take the bus with you when the limo breaks down.
Oprah Winfrey

Friends come and go, but enemies accumulate.
Thomas Jones

The imaginary friends I had as a kid dropped me because their friends thought I didn't exist.
Aaron Machado

It is important for our friends to believe that we are unreservedly frank with them, and important to friendship that we are not.
Mignon McLaughlin

Friendship is not possible between two women, one of whom is very well dressed.
Laurie Colwin

You want a friend in Washington? Get a dog.
Harry S. Truman

Do I not destroy my enemies when I make them my friends?
Abraham Lincoln

A true friend is one who overlooks your failures and tolerates your success
Doug Larson

Two people are never such good friends as when they share a mutual dislike of a third person.
Anon

If your friends don't make fun of you, they're not really your friends.
Anon

Between friends, differences in taste or opinion are irritating in direct proportion to their triviality.
W.H. Auden

Friendship is like money, easier made than kept.
Samuel Butler

It's the friends you can call up at 4 a.m. that matter.
Marlene Dietrich

Marriage: A friendship recognized by the police.
Robert Louis Balfour Stevenson

Don't tell your friends about your indigestion. "How are you" is a greeting, not a question.
Arthur Guiterman

One good reason to only maintain a small circle of friends is that three out of four murders are committed by people who know the victim.
George Carlin

The proper office of a friend is to side with you when you are wrong. Nearly anybody will side with you when you are right.
Mark Twain

I have lost friends, some by death, others through sheer inability to cross the street.
Virginia Woolf

CHAPTER 11: GOVERNMENT

The government's view of the economy could be summed up in a few short phrases: If it moves, tax it. If it keeps moving, regulate it. And if it stops moving, subsidize it.
Ronald Reagan

I've heard that the government wants to put a tax on the mathematically ignorant. Funny, I thought that's what the lottery was
Gallagher

The best government is a benevolent tyranny tempered by an occasional assassination.
Voltaire

The primary function of the government is - and here I am quoting directly from the U.S. Constitution - "to spew out paper."
Dave Barry

A government that robs Peter to pay Paul can always depend on the support of Paul.
George Bernard Shaw

Ask not what the government can do for you. Ask why it doesn't.
Gerhard Kocher

Strange women lying in ponds distributing swords is no basis for a system of government.
Monty Python and the Holy Grail

The best argument against democracy is a five-minute conversation with the average voter.
Winston Churchill

I don't make jokes. I just watch the government and report the facts.
Will Rogers

Outside the killings Washington has one of the lowest crime rates in the country.
Mayor Marion Barry

A fool and his money are soon elected.
Will Rogers

The most terrifying words in the English language are: I'm from the government and I'm here to help.
Ronald Reagan

The problem with socialism is that you eventually run out of other peoples' money.
Margaret Thatcher

Democracy is the art and science of running the circus from the monkey cage.
H. L. Mencken

A government big enough to give you everything you want is a government big enough to take from you everything you have.
Gerald R. Ford

Democracy is a device that ensures we shall be governed no better than we deserve.
George Bernard Shaw

We hang the petty thieves and appoint the great ones to public office.
Aesop

How come we choose from just two people to run for president and fifty for Miss America?
Anon

Democracy must be something more than two wolves and a sheep voting on what to have for dinner.
James Bovard

If voting made any difference they wouldn't let us do it.
Mark Twain

Winston Smith: Does Big Brother exist?
O'Brien: Of course he exists.
Winston Smith: Does he exist like you or me?
O'Brien: You do not exist.
George Orwell

A diplomat is someone who can tell you to go to hell in such a way that you will look forward to the trip.
Azgraybebly Joslan

CHAPTER 12: HAPPINESS

Some cause happiness wherever they go; others, whenever they go.
Oscar Wilde

One of the keys to happiness is a bad memory.
Rita Mae Brown

If I could drop dead right now, I'd be the happiest man alive.
Sam Goldwyn

The advantage of a bad memory is that one enjoys several times the same good things for the first time.
Friedrich Nietzsche

Happiness is having a large, loving, caring, close-knit family in another city.
George Burns

Happiness? That's nothing more than a good health and a poor memory.
Albert Schweitzer

Money can't buy you happiness but it does bring you a more pleasant form of misery.
Spike Milligan

Happiness: an agreeable sensation arising from contemplating the misery of another.
Ambrose Bierce

They say money can't buy happiness but you can buy pizza, cake, candy and Netflix, so they're lying.
Anon

A man doesn't know what happiness is until he's married. By then it's too late.

Frank Sintara

Happiness equals reality minus expectations

Tom Magliozzi

To be happy with a man you must understand him a lot and love him a little. To be happy with a woman you must love her a lot and not try to understand her at all.

Helen Rowland

Money doesn't make you happy. I now have $50 million but I was just as happy when I had $48 million.

Arnold Schwarzenegger

All marriages are happy. It's the living together afterward that causes all the trouble.

Raymond Hull

A happy life is one spent in learning, earning, and yearning.

Lillian Gish

Happiness is an agreeable sensation arising from contemplating the misery of another.

Ambrose Bierce

No pleasure is worth giving up for two more years in a geriatric home in Weston super Mare.

Kingsley Amis

Happiness is good health and a bad memory.

Ingrid Bergman

CHAPTER 13: HUMAN NATURE

Patience is something you admire in the driver behind you, but not in one ahead.
Bill McGlashen

Most people are only alive because it's illegal to shoot them.
Anon

Controversy equalizes fools and wise men ... and the fools know it.
Oliver Wendell Holmes Jr

It's true hard work never killed anybody, but I figure, why take the chance?
Ronald Reagan

The trouble with being punctual is that nobody's there to appreciate it.
Franklin P Jones

I hate housework! You make the beds, you do the dishes–and six months later you have to start all over again.
Joan Rivers

Tell a man there are 300 billion stars in the universe and he'll believe you. Tell him a bench has wet paint on it and he'll have to touch it to be sure.
Anon

Accept who you are, unless you're a serial killer.
Ellen Degeneres

I tried to be normal once. Worst two minutes of my life.
Ziad K. Abdelnour

Misers aren't fun to live with, but they make wonderful ancestors.
David Brenner

People say nothing is impossible, but I do nothing every day.
Winnie The Pooh

It's useless to hold a person to anything they say when they are in love, drunk, or running for office.
Shirley MacLaine

I told my psychiatrist that everyone hates me. He said I was being ridiculous - everyone hasn't met me yet.
Rodney Dangerfield.

The greatest lesson in life is to know that even fools are right sometimes.
Winston Churchill

The aim of a joke is not to degrade the human being, but to remind him that he is already degraded.
George Orwell

Fashion is what you adopt when you don't know who you are.
Quentin Crisp

I always wanted to be somebody, but now I realize I should have been more specific.
Lily Tomlin

Clothes make the man. Naked people have little or no influence on society.
Mark Twain

The only normal people are the ones you don't know very well.
Joe Ancis

Look how often the unexpected happens -- yet we still never expect it.
Ashleigh Brilliant

What we learn from history is that people don't learn from history.
Warren Buffet

If you're too open-minded, your brains will fall out.
Lawrence Ferlinghetti

A cynic is a man who, when he smells flowers, looks around for a coffin.
H. L. Mencken

To argue with a person who has renounced the use of reason is like administering medicine to the dead.
Thomas Paine

It is an ironic habit of human beings to run faster when they have lost their way.
Rollo May

CHAPTER 14: INSULTS

I would challenge you to a battle of wits, but I see you are unarmed.
William Shakespeare

Everyone is entitled to be stupid, but some abuse the privilege.
Anon

A modest little person, with much to be modest about.
Winston Churchill

He can compress the most words into the smallest idea of any man I know.
Abraham Lincoln

He has the attention span of a lightning bolt.
Robert Redford

They never open their mouths without subtracting from the sum of human knowledge.
Thomas Brackett Reed

He loves nature in spite of what it did to him.
Forrest Tucker

She is the original good time that was had by all.
Bette Davis

I don't hate you. I just don't like that you exist.
Gena Showalter

I never forget a face, but in your case I'll be glad to make an exception.
Groucho Marx

Mr. Madison, what you've just said is one of the most insanely idiotic things I have ever heard. At no point in your rambling, incoherent response were you even close to anything that could be considered a rational thought. Everyone in this room is now dumber for having listened to it. I award you no points, and may God have mercy on your soul.
Billy Madison

I like half of you half as well as I should like, and I like less than half of you half as well as you deserve!
J.R.R. Tolkien

He has no equal. Everyone else is better.
Jason Q.

You know why you hate me so much, Jeffery? Because I look the way you feel.
Joe Pesci (Simon B. Wilder)

He is one of those people who would be enormously improved by death.
H. H. Munro

I could dance with you until the cows come home... on second thoughts, I'll dance with the cows and you go home.
Groucho Marx

Has it ever occurred to you that there might be a difference between having an open mind and having holes in one's head?
Richard Schultz

Where's your girlfriend? Outside grazing, I presume.
Jo Brand

Don't be humble, you're not that great.
Golda Meir

Ian Botham is in no way inhibited by a capacity to over-intellectualise.
Frances Edmonds

Am reserving two tickets for you for my premiere. Come and bring a friend - if you have one.
George Bernard Shaw to Winston Churchill

Impossible to be present for the first performance. Will attend second - if there is one.
Churchill's reply

Wisdom eventually comes to all of us. Someday it might even be your turn.
David & Leigh Eddings

Shaw writes plays for the ages, the ages between five and twelve.
George Jean Nathan

Ah, Mozart! He was happily married - but his wife wasn't.
Victor Borge

She's so ugly, the tide wouldn't take her out.
Martin Kaye

You wouldn't be intelligent enough to understand anything that I would be stupid enough to tell you anyways.
Bill Merrill

If men's minds were like dominoes, surely his would be the double blank.
P. G. Wodehouse

Dahling, when God put teeth in your mouth, he ruined a perfectly good arsehole.
Neil Gaiman

From the moment I picked your book up until I put it down I was convulsed with laughter. Someday I intend reading it.
Groucho Marx

The trouble with her is that she lacks the power of conversation but not the power of speech.
George Bernard Shaw

He's a real gentleman. I bet he takes the dishes out of the sink before he pees in it.
Shirley Maclaine

Don't think of yourself as an ugly person, think of yourself as a beautiful monkey.
Tanya Bianco

God made man in his own image, and it would be a sad look out for Christians throughout the globe if God looked anything like you!
Blackadder

I don't know anything about this man. Anyhow, I only know two things about him. One is, he has never been in jail, and the other is, I don't know why.
Mark Twain

She's the sort of woman who lives for others – you can tell them by their hunted expression.
CS Lewis

What's on your mind if you will forgive the overstatement.
Fred Allen

If your IQ was any lower, we would have to water you.
Anne Robinson

Dear Randolph, utterly unspoiled by failure.
Noel Coward

I fart in your general direction. Your mother was a hamster and your father smelt of elderberries.
Monty Python

I've met a lot of hard-boiled eggs in my life, but you - you're 20 minutes.
Jan Sterling

I may be drunk, Miss, but in the morning I will be sober and you will still be ugly.
Winston Churchill

He has all the virtues I dislike and none of the vices I admire.
Winston Churchill

CHAPTER 15: JOURNALISM

Generally speaking, the best people nowadays go into journalism, the second best into business, the rubbish into politics and the shits into law.
Auberon Waugh

Rock journalism is people who can't write interviewing people who can't talk for people who can't read.
Frank Zappa

Accuracy to a newspaper is what virtue is to a lady; but a newspaper can always print a retraction.
Adlai E. Stevenson

The difference between literature and journalism is that journalism is unreadable, and literature is not read.
Oscar Wilde

Silence is not only golden; it is seldom misquoted.
Bob Monkhouse

America is a country of inventors, and the greatest of inventors are the newspaper men.
Alexander Graham Bell

Journalism is organized gossip.
Edward Eggleston

The man who reads nothing at all is better educated than the man who reads nothing but newspapers.
Thomas Jefferson

Journalism largely consists of saying "Lord Jones is Dead" to people who never knew that Lord Jones was alive.
Gilbert K. Chesterton

The First Law of Journalism: to confirm existing prejudice, rather than contradict it.
Alexander Cockburn

If you don't read the newspaper, you are uninformed. If you do read the newspaper, you are misinformed.
Mark Twain

If the newspapers of a country are filled with good news, the jails of that country will be filled with good people.
Daniel Moynihan

Journalism could be described as turning one's enemies into money.
Craig Brown

It is difficult to produce a television documentary that is both incisive and probing, when every twelve minutes one is interrupted by twelve dancing rabbits singing about toilet paper.
Rod Serling

News is something someone wants suppressed. Everything else is just advertising.
Lord Northcliff

A news story should be like a mini skirt on a pretty woman. Long enough to cover the subject but short enough to be interesting.
Anon

News is history shot on the wing.
Gene Fowler

The secret of successful journalism is to make your readers so angry they will write half your paper for you.
C.E.M. Joad

Remember, son, many a good story has been ruined by over-verification.
James Gordon Bennett

Freedom of the press in Britain is freedom to print such of the proprietor's prejudices as the advertisers don't object to.
Hannen Swaffer

Wooing the press is an exercise roughly akin to picnicking with a tiger. You might enjoy the meal, but the tiger always eats last.
Maureen Dowd

CHAPTER 16: KNOWLEDGE

Some problems are so complex that you have to be highly intelligent and well informed just to be undecided about them.
Laurence J. Peter

Facts are meaningless. You can use facts to prove anything that's remotely true!
Homer Simpson

Knowledge is knowing a tomato is a fruit; wisdom is not putting it in a fruit salad.
Miles Kington

Do not argue with an idiot. He will drag you down to his level and beat you with experience.
Greg King

If you're not confused, you're not paying attention.
Tom Peters

Nothing sucks more than that moment during an argument when you realize you're wrong.
Anon

Realism is just another name for yesterday's thinking.
Robert Kriegel

The only mystery in life is why the kamikaze pilots wore helmets.
Al McGuire

Never, under any circumstances, take a sleeping pill and a laxative on the same night.
Dave Barry

We've all heard that a million monkeys banging on a million typewriters will eventually reproduce the entire works of Shakespeare. Now, thanks to the Internet, we know this is not true.
Robert Wilensky

Those people who think they know everything are a great annoyance to those of us who do.
Isaac Asimov

A horse that can count to ten is a remarkable horse—not a remarkable mathematician.
Warren Buffett

Two things are infinite, the universe and human stupidity, and I am not yet completely sure about the universe.
Albert Einstein

When everyone thinks alike, no one thinks very much.
Walter Lippmann

A common mistake that people make when trying to design something completely foolproof is to underestimate the ingenuity of complete fools.
Douglas Adams

The conclusion is the place where you got tired of thinking.
Arthur Bloc

Definition of statistics: the science of producing unreliable facts from reliable figures.
Evan Esar

Some drink deeply from the river of knowledge. Some only gargle

Woody Allen

Genius may have its limitations, but stupidity is not thus handicapped.

Elbert Hubbard

It would be nice to be sure of anything the way some people are of everything.

Anon

Sometimes it's better to keep your mouth closed and let people wonder if you're a fool than to open it and remove all their doubt.

Abraham Lincoln

History is a set of lies agreed upon.

Napoleon

CHAPTER 17: LAST WORDS

Why yes - a bulletproof vest.
James Rodges, murderer, on his final request before the firing squad.

My work is done. Why wait?
George Eastman, U.S. inventor and industrialist (his suicide note)

Am I dying or is this my birthday?
Lady Nancy Astor

I should never have switched from Scotch to Martinis.
Humphrey Bogart

I am still alive.
Caligula

God will pardon me, that's his line of work.
Heinrich Heine

I've had eighteen straight whiskies; I think that's the record . . .
Dylan Thomas

I owe much; I have nothing; the rest I leave to the poor.
François Rabelais

Either that wallpaper goes, or I do.
Oscar Wilde

All my possessions for a moment of time.
Elizabeth I

I've never felt better.
Douglas Fairbanks, Sr.

I'd hate to die twice. It's so boring.
Richard Feynman

Go on, get out - last words are for fools who haven't said enough.
Karl Marx

They couldn't hit an elephant at this dist. . . .
General John Sedgwick

Don't let it end like this. Tell them I said something.
Pancho Villa

Curtain. Fast music! Light. Ready for the last finale. Great. The show looks good, the show looks good.
Florenz Ziegfeld

CHAPTER 18: LAW & LAWYERS

When you go into court you are putting your fate into the hands of twelve people who weren't smart enough to get out of jury duty.
Norm Crosby

I used to be a lawyer, but now I am a reformed character.
Woodrow Wilson

You get a reasonable doubt for a reasonable price.
Criminal lawyer saying

Lawyer: An individual whose principal role is to protect his clients from others of his profession.
Anon

Anybody who thinks talk is cheap should get some legal advice.
Franklin P. Jones

Make crime pay. Become a Lawyer.
Will Rogers

Doctors are just the same as lawyers; the only difference is that lawyers merely rob you, whereas doctors rob you and kill you too.
Anton Chekhov

The only thing scarier than Godzilla is Godzilla's lawyers.
Paul Watson

Ignorance of the law excuses no man -- from practicing it.
Adison Mizner

The minute you read something that you can't understand, you can almost be sure that it was drawn up by a lawyer.
Will Rogers

It is better to be a mouse in a cat's mouth than a man in a lawyer's hands.
Spanish Proverb

If you don't get a lawyer who knows law, then get the one who knows the Judge.
Anon

A lawyer with a briefcase can steal more than a thousand men with guns.
Mario Puzo

A jury consists of twelve persons chosen to decide who has the better lawyer.
Robert Frost

Lawyer: One who protects us from robbers by taking away the temptation.
HL Mencken

He who is his own lawyer has a fool for a client.
Proverb

Going to trial with a lawyer who considers your whole life-style a Crime in Progress is not a happy prospect.
Hunter S. Thompson

To some lawyers, all facts are created equal.
Felix Frankfurter

Lawyers spend a great deal of their time shoveling smoke.
Oliver Wendell Holmes, Jr.

Lawyers are like rhinoceroses: thick skinned, short-sighted, and always ready to charge.
David Mellor

A good lawyer makes you believe the truth but a great lawyer makes you believe in the lie.
Anon

Judge - A law student who marks his own examination papers.
HL Mencken

I learned law so well, the day I graduated I sued the college, won the case, and got my tuition back.
Fred Allen

CHAPTER 19: LIFE

Worry is like a rocking chair: it gives you something to do but never gets you anywhere.
Erma Bombeck

My life has been filled with terrible misfortune; most of which never happened.
Montaigne

As I am becoming older, the only thing that speeds up is time.
Alan Alda

Life is pleasant. Death is peaceful. It's the transition that's troublesome.
Isaac Asimov

I came from a real tough neighborhood. Once a guy pulled a knife on me. I knew he wasn't a professional, the knife had butter on it.
Rodney Dangerfield

In life, it's not who you know that's important, it's how your wife found out.
Joey Adams

It may be that your sole purpose in life is simply to serve as a warning to others.
Anon

We live in a society where pizza gets to your house before the police.
Anon

Life is full of misery, loneliness, and suffering - and it's all over much too soon.
Woody Allen

Always remember that you are absolutely unique. Just like everyone else.
Margaret Mead

The very purpose of existence is to reconcile the glowing opinion we hold of ourselves with the appalling things that other people think about us.
Quentin Crisp

The problem with life is, by the time you can read women like a book, your library card has expired.
Milton Berle

It's not that life is so short.... It's that you're dead so long.
Mark Whetu

You want to look younger. Rent smaller children.
Phyllis Diller

The secret to life is to be older than your lawn.
Franklin's grandfather (Peanuts comic strip)

Forty is the old age of youth. Fifty is the youth of old age.
Victor Hugo

A worm hole is a tunnel at the end of the light.
Rudolf Rab

I don't believe in astrology; I'm a Sagittarian and we're skeptical.
Arthur C. Clarke

Crowded elevators smell different to midgets.
Anon

We only have to look at ourselves to see how intelligent life might develop into something we wouldn't want to meet.
Stephen Hawking

The only way to get rid of a temptation is to yield to it.
 Oscar Wilde

Do not take life too seriously. You will never get out of it alive.
Elbert Hubbard

The old believe everything, the middle aged suspect everything, the young know everything.
Oscar Wilde

The past is an old armchair in the attic, the present an ominous ticking sound, and the future is anybody's guess.
James Thurber

If you can keep your head when all about you are losing theirs, it's just possible you haven't grasped the situation.
Jean Kerr

You can't fix stupid.
Larry Morgan

The grass is always greener over the septic tank.
Erma Bombeck

CHAPTER 20: LITERATURE

One of the great things about books is sometimes there are some fantastic pictures.
George W. Bush

Always read something that will make you look good if you die in the middle of it.
P.J. O'Rourke

I love deadlines. I like the whooshing sound they make as they fly by.
Doulas Adams

Isn't it interesting that the same people who laugh at science fiction listen to weather forecasts and economists?
Kelvin Throop III

Leisure without literature is death and burial alive.
Seneca

The man who doesn't read good books has no advantage over the man who can't read them.
Mark Twain

I wrote a few children's books... not on purpose.
Stephen Wright

The books that everybody admires are those that nobody reads.
Anatole France

When I was your age, television was called books.
The Princess Bride

And therefore education at the University mostly worked by the age-old method of putting a lot of young people in the vicinity of a lot of books and hoping that something would pass from one to the other, while the actual young people put themselves in the vicinity of inns and taverns for exactly the same reason.

Terry Pratchett

I took a speed-reading course and read War and Peace in twenty minutes. It involves Russia.

Woody Allen

An author is a fool who, not content with boring those he lives with, insists on boring future generations.

Charles De Montesquieu.

One trouble with developing speed reading skills is that by the time you realise a book is boring you have finished it..

George W. Bush

CHAPTER 21: LOVE

Love is like an hourglass, with the heart filling up as the brain empties.
Jules Renard

By all means, marry. If you get a good wife, you'll become happy; if you get a bad one, you'll become a philosopher.
Socrates

Men have only two emotions: hungry and horny. If you see him without an erection, make him a sandwich.
Anon

Love conquers all things except poverty and toothache.
Mae West

Falling in love consists merely in uncorking the imagination and bottling the common sense.
Helen Rowland

Love is temporary insanity curable by marriage.
Ambrose Bierce

Love is blind but marriage is a real eye-opener.
Pauline Thomason

Men always want to be a woman's first love - women like to be a man's last romance.
Oscar Wilde

Love is a fire. But whether it is going to warm your hearth or burn down your house, you can never tell.
Joan Crawford

Women are meant to be loved, not to be understood.
Oscar Wilde

First love is a kind of vaccination which saves man from catching the complaint the second time.
Honore de Balzac

A pair of powerful spectacles has sometimes sufficed to cure a person in love.
Friedrich Nietzsche

A youth with his first cigar makes himself sick. A youth with his first girl makes everybody sick.
Mary Wilson

Love sucks. Sometimes it feels good. Sometimes it's just another way to bleed.
Laurell K. Hamilton

Love is only a dirty trick played on us to achieve continuation of the species.
W. Somerset Maugham

You can't put a price tag on love. But if you could, I'd wait for it to go on sale.
Hussein Nishah

If loving someone is putting them in a straitjacket and kicking them down a flight of stairs, then yes, I have loved a few people.
Jarod Kintz

Love is like war, easy to begin but hard to end.
Leo Buscaglia

Love thy neighbor — and if he happens to be tall, debonair and devastating, it will be that much easier.
Mae West

Love is the thing that enables a woman to sing while she mops up the floor after her husband has walked across it in his barn boots.
Anon

Nothing takes the taste out of peanut butter quite like unrequited love.
Charlie Brown

It is easier to love humanity as a whole than to love one's neighbor.
Eric Hoffer

If love is blind, why is lingerie so popular?
Anon

Bart! With ten thousand dollars, we'd be millionaires! We could buy all kinds of useful things like... love!
Homer Simpson

A guy knows he's in love when he loses interest in his car for a couple of days.
Tim Allen

Love is a lot like a backache, it doesn't show up on X-rays, but you know it's there.
George Burns

You can't buy love, but you can pay heavily for it
Henny Youngman

Women still remember the first kiss after men have forgotten the last.
Remy de Gourmont

Any husband who says, "My wife and I are completely equal partners," is talking about either a law firm or a hand of bridge.
Bill Cosby

To be in love is merely to be in a state of perceptual anesthesia.
H.L. Mencken

Three things can't be hidden: coughing, poverty, and love.
Yiddish proverb

If you do kiss a politician, remember this: You are not only kissing him, you are kissing every butt that he has kissed in the last eight years.
Jay Leno

Don't allow someone to be your priority while allowing yourself to be there option.
Mark Twain

The greatest love is a mother's; then a dog's; then a sweetheart's.
Polish proverb

Love is like a game of chess: One false move and you're mated.
Anon

CHAPTER 22: MARRIAGE

The poor wish to be rich, the rich wish to be happy, the single wish to be married and the married wish to be dead.
Ann Landers

Instead of getting married again, I'm going to find a woman I don't like and just give her a house.
Rod Stewart

I was married by a judge. I should have asked for a jury.
Groucho Marx

Marriage is really tough because you have to deal with feelings and lawyers.
Richard Pryor

No man is truly married until he understands every word his wife is not saying.
Anon

In Hollywood a marriage is a success if it outlasts milk.
Rita Rudner

I haven't spoken to my wife in years. I didn't want to interrupt her.
Rodney Dangerfield

I think men who have a pierced ear are better prepared for marriage. They've experienced pain and bought jewelry.
Rita Rudner

When a man opens the door of his car for his wife, you can be sure of one thing: either the car is new or the wife is.
Thomas C Halliburton

Men marry women with the hope they will never change. Women marry men with the hope they will change. And they are both disappointed.
Albert Einstein

The secret of a happy marriage remains a secret.
Henry Youngman

The proper basis for a marriage is mutual misunderstanding.
Oscar Wilde

Getting married is a lot like getting into a tub of hot water. After you get used to it, it ain't so hot.
Minnie Pearl

Behind every great man there is a surprised woman.
Maryon Pearson

Just because nobody complains doesn't mean all parachutes are perfect.
Benny Hill

This would be a much better world if more married couples were as deeply in love as they are in debt.
Earl Wilson

The way taxes are, you might as well marry for love.
Joe Louis

A fool and her money are soon courted.
Helen Rowland

My husband said he needed more space. So I locked him outside.
Roseanne Barr

Marriage is an attempt to solve problems together you didn't even had when you were on your own..
Eddie Cantor

An archaeologist is the best husband a woman can have; the older she gets the more interested he is in her.
Agatha Christie

Marry a man your own age; as your beauty fades, so will his eyesight.
Phyllis Diller

I told my wife the truth. I told her I was seeing a psychiatrist. Then she told me the truth: that she was seeing a psychiatrist, two plumbers, and a bartender.
Rodney Dangerfield

To keep your marriage brimming, with love in the loving cup, whenever you're wrong admit it; whenever you're right shut up.
Ogden Nash

I've had bad luck with both my wives. The first one left me and the second one didn't.
Patrick Murray

My brother is gay and my parents don't care, as long as he marries a doctor.
Elayne Boosler

I'm single by choice. Not my choice.
Orny Adams

A husband is what is left of the lover after the nerve has been extracted.
Helen Rowland

A man is incomplete until he is married. After that, he is finished.
Zsa Zsa Gabor

Marriage is a three ring circus: engagement ring, wedding ring, and suffering.
Aeschylus

Marriage is a lot like the army, everyone complains, but you'd be surprise at the large number that re-enlist.
James Garner

If you want to sacrifice the admiration of many men for the criticism of one, go ahead, get married.
Katharine Hepburn

Many a man in love with a dimple makes the mistake of marrying the whole thing.
Stephen Leacock

Marriage is the triumph of imagination over intelligence. Second marriage is the triumph of hope over experience.
Oscar Wilde

If you want your wife to listen to you, then talk to another woman; she'll be all ears.
Sigmund Freud

In the sex war, thoughtlessness is the weapon of the male, vindictiveness of the female.
Cyril Connolly

Marriage is the only war in which you sleep with the enemy.
French Proverb

Husbands are like fires - they go out when they're left unattended.
Cher

CHAPTER 23: MEN

No man is totally useless - he can always serve as a bad example.
Anon

Call me old fashioned but I tend to think of people with penises as men.
Ian McEwan

Men are only as loyal as their options.
Bill Maher

I can resist everything except temptation –
Oscar Wilde

Men aren't necessities, they're luxuries.
Cher

Every man is thoroughly happy twice in his life: just after he has met his first love, and just after he has left his last one.
Henry Louis Mencken

Coffee, Chocolate, Men. The richer the better!
Anon

When women are depressed, they eat or go shopping. Men invade another country. It's a whole different way of thinking.
Elayne Boosler

Men are like chocolate bars...they're sweet and smooth but head straight for your hips.
Nikki Nicole

What would men be without women? Scarce, sir...mighty scarce.
Mark Twain

Here's all you have to know about men and women: women are crazy, men are stupid. And the main reason women are crazy is that men are stupid.
George Carlin

A man's face is his autobiography. A woman's face is her work of fiction.
Oscar Wilde

The ideal man goes home early, doesn't flirt, doesn't drink, doesn't smoke, doesn't gamble and doesn't exist.
Anon

The greatest deception men suffer is from their own opinions.
Leonardo da Vinci

See, the problem is that God gives men a brain and a penis, and only enough blood to run one at a time.
Robin Williams

Men have a much better time of it than women. For one thing, they marry later, for another thing, they die earlier.
H. L. Mencken

Can you imagine a world without men? No crime and lots of happy fat women.
Nicole Hollander

I want a man whose kind and understanding. Is that too much to ask of a millionaire?
Zsa Zsa Gabor

A lot of guys think the larger a woman's breasts are, the less intelligent she is. I don't think it works like that. I think it's the opposite. I think the larger a woman's breasts are, the less intelligent the men become.
Anita Wise

Why do men chase women they have no intention of marrying? The same urge that makes dogs chase cars they have no intention of driving.
Anon

A man who marries his mistress leaves a vacancy in that position.
Oscar Wilde

When a man steals your wife there is no better revenge than to let him keep her.
Sacha Guitry

When a man brings his wife flowers for no reason, there's a reason.
Molly McGee

Men are like bank accounts. Without a lot of money they don't generate a lot of interest.
Anon

The quickest way to a man's heart is through his chest.
Roseanne Barr

A man in love is like a clipped coupon - it's time to cash in.
Mae West

The useless piece of flesh at the end of a penis is called a man.
Jo Brand

A hard man is good to find.
Mae West

Macho does not prove mucho.
Zsa Zsa Gabor

That is the great distinction between the sexes. Men see objects, women see the relationships between objects.
John Fowles

CHAPTER 24: MONEY

The most popular labor-saving device is still money.
Phyllis George

Successful Investing takes time, discipline and patience. No matter how great the talent or effort, some things just take time: You can't produce a baby in one month by getting nine women pregnant.
Warren Buffet

Advertising may be described as the science of arresting the human intelligence long enough to get money from it.
Stephen Leacock

A stockbroker urged me to buy a stock that would triple its value every year. I told him, "At my age, I don't even buy green bananas".
Claude Pepper

All I ask is the chance to prove that money can't make me happy.
Spike Milligan

Acquaintance, n.: A person whom we know well enough to borrow from, but not well enough to lend to.
Ambrose Bierce

When you've got them by their wallets, their hearts and minds will follow.
Fern Naito

There were times my pants were so thin I could sit on a dime and tell if it was heads or tails.
Spencer Tracy

If you're given a choice between money and sex appeal, take the money. As you get older, the money will become your sex appeal.
Katherine Hepburn

I'm living so far beyond my income that we may almost be said to be living apart.
e e cummings

People say that money is not the key to happiness, but I always figured if you have enough money, you can have a key made.
Joan Rivers

I buy expensive suits. They just look cheap on me.
Warren Buffett

My problem lies in reconciling my gross habits with my net income.
Errol Flynn

Money won't make you happy... but everybody wants to find out for themselves.
Zig Ziglar

Money won is twice as sweet as money earned.
Eddie Felson

Every day I get up and look through the Forbes list of the richest people in America. If I'm not there, I go to work.
Robert Orben

Always borrow money from a pessimist. He won't expect it back.
Oscar Wilde

An accountant is someone who solves a problem you didn't know you had in a way you don't understand.

Anon

Money frees you from doing things you dislike. Since I dislike doing nearly everything, money is handy.

Groucho Marx

A fine is a tax for doing wrong. A tax is a fine for doing well.

Anon

The avoidance of taxes is the only intellectual pursuit that carries any reward.

John Maynard Keynes

Today, it takes more brains and effort to make out the income-tax form than it does to make the income.

Alfred E. Neuman

Next to being shot at and missed, nothing is really quite as satisfying as an income tax refund.

F.J. Raymond

When it's a question of money, everybody is of the same religion.

Voltaire

If you lend someone 20 dollars and never see that person again, it's probably worth it.

Sam Ewing

Money can't buy love, but it improves your bargaining position.

Christopher Marlowe

Dear Lord, help me to break even. I need the money.

Anon

CHAPTER 25: MUSIC

One good thing about music, when it hits you, you feel no pain.
Bob Marley

All music is folk music. I ain't never heard a horse sing a song.
Louis Armstrong

When I was a little boy, I told my dad, 'When I grow up, I want to be a musician.' My dad said: 'You can't do both, Son'.
Chet Atkins

To achieve great things, two things are needed: a plan and not quite enough time.
Leonard Bernstein

In order to compose, all you need to do is remember a tune that nobody else has thought of.
Robert Schumann

There are two kinds of artists left: those who endorse Pepsi and those who simply won't.
Annie Lennox

There's nothing like the eureka moment of knock off a song which didn't exist before – I won't compare it to sex but it lasts longer.
Paul McCartney

Lesser artists borrow, great artists steal.
Igor Stravinsky

It's easy to play any musical instrument: all you have to do is touch the right key at the right time and the instrument will play itself.

Johann Sebastian Bach

Jazz is not dead, it just smells funny.

Frank Zappa

Let me be clear about this: I don't have a drug problem, I have a police problem.

Keith Richards

Talking about music is like dancing about architecture.

Anon

Opera is when a guy gets stabbed in the back and, instead of bleeding, he sings.

Robert Benchley

A painter paints pictures on canvas. But musicians paint their pictures on silence.

Leopold Stokowski

Dancing: The vertical expression of a horizontal desire legalized by music.

George Bernard Shaw

CHAPTER 26: PETS

Dogs have masters. Cats have staff.

Anon

You know what I like most about people? Pets.

Jarod Kintz

In order to keep a true perspective of one's importance, everyone should have a dog that will worship him and a cat that will ignore him.

Dereke Bruce

You can trust your dog to guard your house but never trust your dog to guard your sandwich.

Anon

You can say any foolish thing to a dog, and the dog will give you a look that says, 'Wow, you're right! I never would've thought of that!'

Dave Barry

A dog teaches a boy fidelity, perseverance, and to turn around three times before lying down.

Robert Benchley

To his dog, every man is Napoleon; hence the constant popularity of dogs.

Aldous Huxley

If you think dogs can't count, try putting three dog biscuits in your pocket and then give him only two of them.

Phil Pastoret

I wonder if other dogs think poodles are members of a weird religious cult.
Rita Rudner

A well-trained dog will make no attempt to share your lunch. He will just make you feel so guilty that you cannot enjoy it.
Helen Thomson

My goal in life is to become as wonderful as my dog thinks I am.
Anon

Always remember, a cat looks down on man, a dog looks up to man, but a pig will look man right in the eye and see his equal.
Winston Churchill

If skill could be gained by watching, every dog would become a butcher.
Turkish proverb

The clever cat eats cheese and breathes down rat holes with baited breath.
WC Fields

Dogs come when they're called. Cats take a message and get back to you.
Mary Bly

In order to really enjoy a dog, one doesn't merely train him to be semi-human. The point of it is to open oneself up to the possibility of becoming partly a dog
Edward Hoagland

My favorite animal is steak.
Fran Lebowitz

Dogs believe they are human. Cats believe they are God.

Anon

CHAPTER 27: PHILOSOPHY

For some strange reason, no matter where I go, the place is always called "here".
Ashleigh Brilliant

I am nobody. Nobody is perfect. Therefore, I am perfect.
Anon

If you can remain calm, you don't have all the facts.
Anon

The main thing is keeping the main thing the main thing.
German Proverb

Those who dance are considered insane by those who cannot hear the music.
George Carlin

Nobody goes where the crowds are anymore. It's too crowded.
Yogi Berra

No, I don't have a solution, but I certainly admire the problem.
Ashleigh Brilliant

Did you ever walk in a room and forget why you walked in? I think that's how dogs spend their lives.
Sue Murphy

Give a man a match, and he'll be warm for a minute, but set him on fire, and he'll be warm for the rest of his life.
Terry Pratchett

I took a test in Existentialism. I left all the answers blank and got 100.
Woody Allen

We demand rigidly defined areas of doubt and uncertainty.
Douglas Adams

Risk means 'shit happens' or 'good luck'.
Toba Beta

When in doubt, be ridiculous.
Sherwood Smith

It is not certain that everything is uncertain.
Blaise Pascal

Think left and think right and think low and think high. Oh, the thinks you can think up if only you try.
Dr. Seuss

A concept is a brick. It can be used to build a courthouse of reason. Or it can be thrown through the window.
Gilles Deleuze

Wisest is she who knows she does not know.
Jostein Gaarder

I would never die for my beliefs because I might be wrong.
Bertrand Russell

On the whole human beings want to be good, but not too good, and not quite all the time.
George Orwell

A philosopher is a blind man in a cellar at midnight looking for a black cat which isn't there. He is distinguished from a theologian, in that the theologian finds the cat.
Anon

Hegel set out his philosophy with so much obscurity that people thought it must be profound.
Bertrand Russell

Philosophers before Kant had a tremendous advantage over philosophers after Kant in that they didn't have to waste time studying Kant.
Bertrand Russell

I have come to the conclusion, after many years of sometimes sad experience, that you cannot come to any conclusion at all.
Vita Sackville West

Reality is a collective hunch.
Lily Tomlin

CHAPTER 28: POLITICS

Politics is supposed to be the second oldest profession. I have come to realize that it bears a very close resemblance to the first.
Ronald Reagan

Politicians and diapers have one thing in common. They should both be changed regularly, and for the same reason.
José Maria de Eça de Queiroz

If you can't convince them, confuse them.
Harry S. Truman

My idea of an agreeable person is a person who agrees with me.
Benjamin Disraeli

Politicians who complain about the media are like sailors who complain about the sea.
Enoch Powell

If you're listening to a rock star to get your information on who to vote for, you're a bigger moron than they are.
Alice Cooper

Politics is the conduct of public affairs for private advantage.
Ambrose Bierce

Any 20 year-old who isn't a liberal doesn't have a heart, and any 40 year-old who isn't a conservative doesn't have a brain.
Winston Churchill

Politics is the art of postponing decisions until they are no longer relevant.
Henri Queuille

Politics is the art of looking for trouble, finding it, misdiagnosing it, and then misapplying the wrong remedies.
Groucho Marx

Politics is just show business for ugly people.
Jay Leno

Those who are too smart to engage in politics are punished by being governed by those who are dumber.
Plato

This is an impressive crowd: the Have's and Have-more's. Some people call you the elites. I call you my base.
George W. Bush

Politics, n: Poly "many" + tics "blood-sucking parasites".
Larry Hardiman

All the contact I have had with politics has left me feeling as though I had been drinking out of spittoons.
Ernest Hemingway

The trouble with radicals is that they only read radical literature, and the trouble with conservatives is that they don't read anything.
Thomas Nixon Carver

In politics stupidity is not a handicap.
Napoleon Bonaparte

Conservatives are not necessarily stupid, but most stupid people are conservatives.

John Stuart Mill

Politics is the gentle art of getting votes from the poor and campaign funds from the rich by promising to protect each from the other.

Oscar Ameringer

Politics ain't worrying this country one-tenth as much as where to find a parking space.

Will Rogers

He who believes that the past cannot be changed has not yet written his memoirs.

Torvald Gahli

Politicians were mostly people who'd had too little morals and ethics to stay lawyers.

George R.R. Martin

One picture is worth 1,000 denials.

Ronald Reagan

CHAPTER 29: RELIGION

Going to church doesn't make you a Christian any more than standing in a garage makes you a car.
Billy Sunday

When people talk to God, it's called prayer. When God talks back, it's called schizophrenia.
Fox Mulder

The "bishop" came to my church today, that guy was an imposter, he never once moved diagonally
Anon

I'm normally not a praying man, but if you're up there, please save me Superman.
Homer Simpson

The truths of religion are never so well understood as by those who have lost their power of reasoning.
Voltaire

When I told the people of Northern Ireland that I was an atheist, a woman in the audience stood up and said, 'Yes, but is it the God of the Catholics or the God of the Protestants in whom you don't believe?
Quentin Crisp

Give a man a fish, and you'll feed him for a day; give him a religion, and he'll starve to death while praying for a fish.
Timothy Jones

Morality is doing what is right, no matter what you are told. Religion is doing what you are told, no matter what is right.
HL Mencken

Anyone who thinks sitting in church can make you a Christian must also think that sitting in a garage can make you a car.
Garrison Keillor

Religion is regarded by the common people as true, by the wise as false, and by the rulers as useful.
Seneca

Life in Lubbock, Texas, taught me two things: One is that God loves you and you're going to burn in hell. The other is that sex is the most awful, filthy thing on earth and you should save it for someone you love.
Butch Hancock

The price of freedom of religion, or of speech, or of the press, is that we must put up with a good deal of rubbish.
Robert Jackson

Everybody wants to go to heaven, but nobody wants to die.
Joe Louis

Most people would like to be delivered from temptation but would like it to keep in touch.
Robert Orben

I find it puzzling that those who describe Evolution as "Just A Theory" propose Creationism as an alternative even though it is "Just a Superstition".
Gnossos

God has no religion.
Mahatma Gandhi

Man cannot make a worm, yet he will make gods by the dozen.
Michel Eyquem de Montaigne

My concern is not whether God is on our side; my greatest concern is to be on God's side, for God is always right.
Abraham Lincoln

I always distrust people who know so much about what God wants them to do to their fellows.
Susan B. Anthony

People who want to share their religious views with you, almost never want you to share yours with them.
Dave Barry

An Inuit hunter asked the local missionary priest: "If I did not know about God and sin, would I go to hell?" "No," said the priest, "not if you did not know." "Then why," asked the Inuit earnestly, "did you tell me?"
Annie Dillard

We must respect the other fellow's religion, but only in the sense and to the extent that we respect his theory that his wife is beautiful and his children smart.
Henry Louis Mencken

Religion has done love a great service by making it a sin.
Anatole France

Yes, reason has been a part of organized religion, ever since two nudists took dietary advice from a talking snake.
Jon Stewart

I'm completely in favor of the separation of Church and State.... These two institutions screw us up enough on their own, so both of them together is certain death.
George Carlin

Most people have some sort of religion, at least they know which church they're staying away from.
John Erskine

Every religion in the world that has destroyed people is based on love.
Anton LaVey

The only good thing ever to come out of religion was the music.
George Carlin

I believe there is something out there watching over us. Unfortunately, it's the government.
Woody Allen

Faith is not a function of stupidity but a frequent cause of it.
Wendy Kaminer

If it turns out that there is a God, I don't think that he's evil. But the worst that you can say about him is that basically he's an underachiever.
Woody Allen

CHAPTER 30: SCIENCE

The scientific theory I like best is that the rings of Saturn are composed entirely of lost airline luggage.
Mark Russell

When you are courting a nice girl an hour seems like a second. When you sit on a red-hot cinder a second seems like an hour. That's relativity.
Albert Einstein

If people do not believe that mathematics is simple, it is only because they do not realize how complicated life is.
John Von Neuman

If you try and take a cat apart to see how it works, the first thing you have on your hands is a non-working cat.
Douglas Adams

The generation of random numbers is too important to be left to chance.
Robert Covey

A mathematician is a blind man in a dark room looking for a black cat which isn't there.
Charles R. Darwin

Science operates according to a law of conservation of difficulty. The simplest questions have the hardest answers; to get an easier answer, you need to ask a more complicated question.
George Musser

Nothing travels faster than the speed of light with the possible exception of bad news, which obeys its own special laws.
Douglas Adams

When you get right down to it, almost every explanation Man came up with for anything until about 1926 was stupid.
Dave Barry

If we knew what it was we were doing, it would not be called research, would it?
Albert Einstein

In the beginning the Universe was created. This has made a lot of people very angry and been widely regarded as a bad move.
Douglas Adams, The Hitchhiker's Guide to the Galaxy

An important scientific innovation rarely makes its way by gradually winning over and converting its opponents: What does happen is that the opponents gradually die out.
Max Planck

Science is the record of dead religions.
Oscar Wilde

Sometimes I think the surest sign that intelligent life exists elsewhere in the universe is that none of it has tried to contact us.
Bill Watterson

If math was taught like science in Kansas, Texas, and Tennessee, then 2+2=5 would be a "competing theory."
Anon

Science is organized common sense where many a beautiful theory was killed by an ugly fact.
Thomas Huxley

A fact is a simple statement that everyone believes. It is innocent, unless found guilty. A hypothesis is a novel suggestion that no one wants to believe. It is guilty, until found effective.
Edward Teller

If it's green or wriggles, it's biology.
If it stinks, it's chemistry.
If it doesn't work, it's physics.
Handy Guide to Science

CHAPTER 31: SEX

Bisexuality immediately doubles your chances for a date on Saturday night.
Rodney Dangerfield

To attract men, I wear a perfume called New Car Interior.
Rita Rudner

Women should look good. Work on yourselves. Education? I spit on education. No man is ever going to put his hand up your dress looking for a library card.
Joan Rivers

If you think you are too small to be effective, you have never been in bed with a mosquito.
Bette Reese

It's not true that I had nothing on. I had the radio on.
Marilyn Monroe

Sex education may be a good idea in the schools, but I don't believe the kids should be given homework.
Bill Cosby

Money, it turned out, was exactly like sex, you thought of nothing else if you didn't have it and thought of other things if you did.
James Baldwin

Don't stay in bed, unless you can make money in bed.
George Burns

I'm always looking for meaningful one night stands.
Dudley Moore

Absence diminishes mediocre passions and increases great ones, as the wind extinguishes candles and fans fires.
Francois de La Rochefoucauld

I thought I was promiscuous, but it turns out I was just thorough.
Russell Brand

I'm now making a Jewish porno film. 10 percent sex, 90 percent guilt
Henny Youngman

Honesty is the key to a relationship. If you can fake that, your in.
Richard Jeni

My best birth control now is just to leave the lights on.
Joan Rivers

What a kid I got, I told him about the birds and the bees and he told me about the butcher and my wife.
Rodney Dangerfield

Love is the answer, but while you're waiting for the answer, sex raises some pretty good questions.
Woody Allen

The big difference between sex for money and sex for free is that sex for money usually costs a lot less.
Brendan Behan

There are a number of mechanical devices which increase sexual arousal, particularly in women. Chief among these is the Mercedes-Benz 380SL convertible.
P. J. O'Rourke

The best computer is a man, and it's the only one that can be mass-produced by unskilled labor.
Wernher von Braun

Women need a reason to have sex. Men just need a place.
Billy Crystal

If brevity is the soul of wit, your penis must be a riot.
Donna Gephart

Sex at age 90 is like trying to shoot pool with a rope.
George F Burns

Everything takes longer than it should, except sex.
Murphy's Law

People ask me what I would most like for my eighty seventh birthday. I tell them: a paternity suit.
George Burns

CHAPTER 32: SPORT

If at first you don't succeed . . . so much for skydiving.
Henry Youngman

A computer once beat me at chess, but it was no match for me at kick boxing.
Emo Phillips

I was gonna smack you in the face, but I see God already beat me to it.
Taz (WWF)

If a tie is like kissing your sister, losing is like kissing your grandmother with her teeth out.
George Brett

If defensive linemen's IQs were 5 points lower, they'd be geraniums.
Russ Francis

The only reason I would take up jogging is so that I could hear heavy breathing again.
Erma Bombeck

A critic once characterized baseball as six minutes of action crammed into two-and-one-half hours.
Ray Fitzgerald

The first time I saw Dick Vitale, his hair was blowing in the breeze. And he was too proud to chase it.
Cliff Ellis

I've got to stop this. My entourage is getting entourages.
Jalen Rose

To me, boxing is like a ballet - except there's no music, no choreography, and the dancers hit each other.
Jack Handey

I got into the ring with Muhammad Ali once and I had him worried for a while. He thought he'd killed me!
Tommy Cooper

If they can make penicillin out of mouldy bread, then they can sure make something out of you.
Muhammad Ali

Cricket is a game played by 11 fools and watched by 11,000 fools.
George Bernard Shaw

The third umpires should be changed as often as nappies... and for the same reason.
Navjot Sidhu

Hockey is a sport for white men. Basketball is a sport for black men. Golf is a sport for white men dressed like black pimps.
Tiger Woods

The difference between golf and government is that in golf you can't improve your lie.
George Deukmejian

While playing golf today I hit two good balls. I stepped on a rake.
Henry Youngman

A difference of opinion is what makes horse racing and missionaries.
Will Rogers

Golf is a game whose aim is to hit a very small ball into an even smaller hole, with weapons singularly ill-designed for the purpose.
Winston Churchill

You could remove the brains from 90% of jockeys and they would weigh the same.
John Francome

Ice hockey is a form of disorderly conduct in which the score is kept.
Doug Larson

I never comment on referees and I'm not going to break the habit of a lifetime for that prat.
Ewan McKenzice

Stephen Hendry jumps on Steve Davis' misses every chance he gets.
Mike Hallet

Julian Dicks is everywhere. It's like they've got eleven Dicks on the field.
Metro Radio.

If it weren't for baseball, many kids wouldn't know what a millionaire looked like.
Phyllis Diller

CHAPTER 33: SUCCESS

Success is relative. It is what we can make of the mess we have made of things.
TS Eliot

If at first you don't succeed; you are running about average.
MH Alderson

A successful man is one who makes more money than his wife can spend. A successful woman is one who can find such a man.
Lana Turner

I asked God for a bike, but I know God doesn't work that way. So I stole a bike and asked for forgiveness.
Emo Phillips

Success in almost any field depends more on energy and drive than it does on intelligence. This explains why we have so many stupid leaders.
Sloan Wilson

Wherever I go, people are waving at me. Maybe if I do a good job, they'll use all their fingers.
Frank King

Let us be thankful for the fools. But for them the rest of us could not succeed.
Mark Twain

Anybody can win, unless there happens to be a second entry.
George Ade

Moderation is a fatal thing. Nothing succeeds like excess.
Oscar Wilde

Nothing is so embarrassing as watching someone do something that you said couldn't be done.
Sam Ewing

All you need in this life is ignorance and confidence, and then success is sure.
Mark Twain

If you're not failing every now and again, it's a sign you're not doing anything very innovative.
Woody Allen

Victory goes to the player who makes the next-to-last mistake.
Savielly Grigorievitch Tartakower

Success is simply a matter of luck. Ask any failure.
Earl Wilson

If at first you don't succeed, failure may be your style.
Quentin Crisp

If at first you don't succeed, try, try again. Then quit. There's no point in being a damn fool about it.
WC Fields

The worst part of having success is trying to find someone who is happy for you.
Bette Middler

My formula for success is to rise early, work late and strike oil.
John Paul Getty

Winning is only important in war and surgery.
Al McGuire

You win some, you lose some, and then there is that little known third category.
Al Gore

It is sobering to consider that when Mozart was my age he had already been dead for a year.
Tom Lehrer

Whenever a friend succeeds, a little something in me dies.
Gore Vidal

The penalty of success is to be bored by people who used to snub you.
Lady Astor

Seventy percent of success in life is showing up.
Woody Allen

Chapter 34: Technology

Programming today is a race between software engineers striving to build bigger and better idiot proof programs, and the universe trying to produce bigger and better idiots. So far the universe is winning.
Rich Cook

If the automobile had followed the same development cycle as the computer, a Rolls Royce would today cost $100, get a million miles per gallon, and explode once a year, killing everyone inside.
Robert X Cringely

The digital camera is a great invention because it allows us to reminisce. Instantly.
Demetri Martin

If you can't explain it to a six-year-old, you don't understand it yourself.
Albert Einstein

Computers are like Old Testament gods; lots of rules and no mercy.
Joseph Campbell

A computer lets you make more mistakes faster than any invention in human history - with the possible exceptions of handguns and tequila.
Mitch Ratcliffe

Television is an invention that permits you to be entertained in your living room by people you wouldn't have in your home.
David Frost

The major difference between a thing that might go wrong and a thing that cannot possibly go wrong is that when a thing that cannot possibly go wrong goes wrong it usually turns out to be impossible to get at or repair.
Douglas Adams

Any sufficiently advanced technology is indistinguishable from magic.
Arthur C. Clarke

Computers are useless. They can only give you answers.
Pablo Picasso

We don't care. We don't have to. We're the phone company.
Lily Tomlin

It is a medium of entertainment which permits millions of people to listen to the same joke at the same time, and yet remain lonesome.
T.S. Eliot, about radio

I am sorry to say that there is too much point to the wisecrack that life is extinct on other planets because their scientists were more advanced than ours.
John F. Kennedy

Never trust anything that can think for itself if you can't see where it keeps its brain.
J.K. Rowling

The factory of the future will have only two employees, a man and a dog. The man will be there to feed the dog. The dog will be there to keep the man from touching the equipment.
Warren G. Bennis

Lo! Men have become the tools of their tools.
Henry David Thoreau

Hacking is like sex. You get in, you get out, and hope that you didn't leave something that can be traced back to you.
Anon

The Internet: where men are men, women are men, and children are FBI agents.
Anon

Computers make it easier to do a lot of things, but most of the things they make it easier to do don't need to be done.
Andy Rooney

There are two major products that came out of Berkeley: LSD and UNIX. We don't believe this to be a coincidence.
Jeremy S. Anderson

Foolproof systems don't take into account the ingenuity of fools.
Gene Brown.

Technology is a way of organizing the universe so that man doesn't have to experience it.
Max Frisch

Everything that can be invented has been invented.
Charles H. Duell, Commissioner, U.S. Office of Patents,1899

CHAPTER 35: TRAVEL

I couldn't repair your brakes, so I made your horn louder.
Steven Wright

You know, somebody actually complimented me on my driving today. They left a little note on the windscreen, it said 'Parking Fine'.
Tommy Cooper

If you don't like the way I drive, stay off the sidewalk
Anon

Why do they call it rush hour when nothing moves?
Robin Williams

That's OK. We can walk to the kerb from here.
Woody Allen

I've called my car Flattery because it gets me nowhere.
Henry Youngman

A friend of mine was so fed up with the train delays and cancellations he threw himself on the track. Died of exposure.
Jack Dee

Being in a ship is like being in a jail, with the option of drowning.
Samuel Johnson

I like terra firma. The more firms, the less terra.
George S Kaufman

A man who, beyond the age of 26, finds himself on a bus can count himself as a failure.
Margaret Thatcher

Modern travelling is not travelling at all; it is merely being sent to a place, and very little different from becoming a parcel.
John Ruskin

Be careful! Travel expands the mind and loosens the bowels.
Abraham Verghese

The first condition of understanding a foreign country is to smell it.
Rudyard Kipling

There are only two reasons to sit in the back row of an airplane: Either you have diarrhea, or you're anxious to meet people who do.
Rich Jeni

A tourist is a fellow who drives thousands of miles so he can be photographed standing in front of his car.
Emile Ganest

My fear of flying starts as soon as I buckle myself in and then the guy up front mumbles a few unintelligible words then before I know it I'm thrust into the back of my seat by acceleration that seems way too fast and the rest of the trip is an endless nightmare of turbulence, of near misses. And then the cabbie drops me off at the airport.
Dennis Miller

On a New York subway you get fined for spitting, but you can throw up for nothing.
Lewis Grizzard

I had a prejudice against the British until I discovered that fifty percent of them were female.
Raymond Floyd

Lovers of air travel find it exhilarating to hang poised between the illusion of immortality and the fact of death.
Alexander Chase

I've been to almost as many places as my luggage.
Bob Hope

Spain travel tip: If bathroom genders are indicated by flamingos, the boy flamingo is the one with a hat. I learned this the hard way.
Dave Barry

Denver International Airport has a control tower that sways in the wind. The good thing about it is that it looks perfectly still to the pilots who've been drinking.
Melanie White

In flying, the probability of survival is inversely proportional to the angle of arrival.
Neil Armstrong

How is it that the first piece of luggage on the airport carousel never belongs to anyone?
George Roberts

In Paris they simply stared when I spoke to them in French; I never did succeed in making those idiots understand their own language.
Mark Twain

It can hardly be a coincidence that no language on earth has ever produced the expression, 'As pretty as an airport'.
Douglas Adams

In Mexico, everything on the menu is the same dish. The only difference is the way it's folded.
Billy Connolly

Just got back from a pleasure trip: I took my mother-in-law to the airport.
Henny Youngman

Americans have always been eager for travel, that being how they got to the New World in the first place.
Otto Friedrich

I travel a lot; I hate having my life disrupted by routine.
Caskie Stinnett

Seasickness: at first you are so sick you are afraid you will die, and then you are so sick you are afraid you won't die.
Mark Twain

The whole object of travel is not to set foot on foreign land; it is at last to set foot on one's own country as a foreign land.
G. K. Chesterton

Everywhere is nowhere. When a person spends all his time in foreign travel, he ends by having many acquaintances, but no friends.
Seneca

Travel is the frivolous part of serious lives, and the serious part of frivolous ones.
Anne Sophie Swetchine

I never travel without my diary. One should always have something sensational to read in the train.
Oscar Wilde

A sure cure for seasickness is to sit under a tree.
Spike Milligan

I want to die in my sleep like my grandfather... Not screaming and yelling like the passengers in his car.
Will Shriner

Anybody going slower than you is an idiot, and anyone going faster than you is a maniac.
Ronnie Corbett

CHAPTER 36: TV

Men don't care what's on TV. They only care what else is on TV.
Jerry Seinfeld

TV is chewing gum for the eyes.
Frank Lloyd Wright

I find television very educating. Every time somebody turns on the set, I go into the other room and read a book.
Groucho Marx

Life doesn't imitate art; it imitates bad television.
Woody Allen

Television! Teacher, mother, secret lover.
Homer Simpson

Radio is the theater of the mind; television is the theater of the mindless.
Steve Allen

Don't you wish there was a knob on the TV to turn up the intelligence? There's one marked brightness, but it doesn't work.
Gallagher

The American people love the Home Shoping Network because it's commercial free.
Will Durst

Norwegian television give you the sensation of a coma without the worry and inconvenience.
Bill Bryson

In Russia we had only two channels. Channel One was propaganda. Channel Two consisted of a KGB officer telling you 'Turn back at once to Channel One'.

Yakov Smirnoff

My show is the stupidest on TV. If you are watching it, get a life.

Jerry Springer

CHAPTER 37: WAR

Gentlemen, you can't fight in here. This is the War Room.
Dr Strangelove

In time of war, when truth is so precious, it must be attended by a bodyguard of lies
Winston Churchill

War is when the government tells you who the bad guy is. Revolution is when you decide that for yourself.
Benjamin Franklin

The object of war is not to die for your country but to make the other bastard die for his.
General George S. Patton

War is God's way of teaching Americans geography.
Ambrose Bierce

Before a war, military science seems a real science, like astronomy; but after a war, it seems more like astrology.
Rebecca West

The quickest way of ending a war is to lose it.
George Orwell

The victor will never be asked if he told the truth.
Adolf Hitler

I know not with what weapons World War III will be fought, but World War IV will be fought with sticks and stones.
Albert Einstein

To ensure perfect aim, shoot first and call whatever you hit the target.
Ashleigh Brilliant

The only real diplomacy ever performed by a diplomat is in deceiving their own people after their dumbness has got them into a war.
Will Rogers

It is forbidden to kill; therefore, all murderers are punished unless they kill in large numbers and to the sound of trumpets.
Voltaire

The direct use of force is such a poor solution to any problem, it is generally employed only by small children and large nations.
David Friedman

War: first, one hopes to win; then one expects the enemy to lose; then, one is satisfied that he too is suffering; in the end, one is surprised that everyone has lost.
Karl Kraus

War does not determine who is right — only who is left.
Anon

The nuclear arms race is like two sworn enemies standing waist deep in gasoline, one with three matches, the other with five.
Carl Sagan

We are not retreating—we are advancing in another direction.
General Douglas MacArthur

A prisoner of war is a man who tries to kill you and fails, and then asks you not to kill him.
Winston Churchill

Men like war: they do not hold much sway over birth, so they make up for it with death. Unlike women, men menstruate by shedding other people's blood.
Lucy Ellman

Politics are very much like war. We may even have to use poison gas at times.
Winston Churchill

War is peace.
Freedom is slavery.
Ignorance is strength.
George Orwell, 1984

Military justice is to justice what military music is to music.
Groucho Marx

You can no more win a war than you can win an earthquake.
Jeannette Rankin

Those who live by the sword get shot by those who don't.
Anon

Chapter 38: Wisdom

Beauty isn't worth thinking about; what's important is your mind. You don't want a fifty-dollar haircut on a fifty-cent head.
Garrison Keillor

Wise men talk because they have something to say. Fools talk because they have to say something.
Plato

Men can acquire knowledge, but not wisdom. Some of the greatest fools ever known were learned men.
Spanish Proverb

The only true wisdom is in knowing you know nothing.
Socrates

There is a difference between happiness and wisdom: he that thinks himself the happiest man is really so; but he that thinks himself the wisest is generally the greatest fool.
Francis Bacon

Wisdom doesn't necessarily come with age. Sometimes age just shows up all by itself.
Tom Wilson

The problem with America is stupidity. I'm not saying there should be a capital punishment for stupidity, but why don't we just take the safety labels off of everything and let the problem solve itself?
Anon

The early bird gets the worm, but the second mouse gets the cheese.
Ernst Berg

Ninety per cent of all human wisdom is the ability to mind your own business.
Robert A Heinlein

I'm not young enough to know everything.
J.M. Barrie

I'm not waiting until my hair turns white to become patient and wise. Nope, I'm dying my hair tonight.
Jarod Kintz

Ridicule is the tribute paid to the genius by the mediocrities.
Oscar Wilde

Never argue with an idiot they'll drag you down to their level and beat you through experience.
Katrina

Doesn't expecting the unexpected make the unexpected expected?
Bob Dylan

If everyone is thinking alike, then somebody isn't thinking.
George S Patton

Everything happens for a reason. But sometimes the reason is that you're stupid and you make bad decisions.
Bill Murray

Heroism is the only way to be famous when we have no talent.
Pierre Desproges

People who think they know everything are a great annoyance to those of us who do.
Isaac Asimov

CHAPTER 39: WOMEN

If evolution really works, how come mothers only have two hands?
Milton Berle

Women who seek to be equal with men lack ambition.
Marilyn Monroe

I can't decide whether I'm a good girl wrapped up in a bad girl, or if I'm a bad girl wrapped up in a good girl. And that's how I know I'm a woman.
C. JoyBell C.

A woman's mind is cleaner than a man's: She changes it more often.
Oliver Herford

She got her good looks from her father. He's a plastic surgeon.
Groucho Marx

I wish I had a twin, so I could know what I'd look like without plastic surgery.
Joan Rivers

If a woman tells you she's 20 and looks 16, she's 12. If she tells you she's 26 and looks 26, she's damn near 40.
Chris Rock

Every girl should use what Mother Nature gave her before Father Time takes it away.
Dr. Laurence J. Peter

Any girl can look glamorous. All you have to do is stand still and look stupid.
Hedy Lamarr

There is nothing wrong with a woman welcoming all men's advances as long as they are in cash.
Zsa Zsa Gabor

Curve: The loveliest distance between two points.
Mae West

Ah, women. They make the highs higher and the lows more frequent.
Friedrich Nietzsche

When women kiss it always reminds me of prize fighters shaking hands.
H.L. Mencken

Home is the girl's prison and the woman's workhouse.
George Bernard Shaw

If women didn't exist, all the money in the world would have no meaning.
Aristotle Onassis

The man's desire is for the woman; but the woman's desire is rarely other than for the desire of the man.
Samuel Taylor Coleridge

Every woman should have four pets in her life. A mink in her closet, a jaguar in her garage, a tiger in her bed, and a jackass who pays for everything.
Paris Hilton

I speak two languages: English and Body.
Mae West

If you want something said, ask a man; if you want something done, ask a woman.
Margaret Thatcher

To be happy with a man you must understand him a lot and love him a little. To be happy with a woman you must love her a lot and not try to understand her at all.
Helen Rowland

Whatever women do, they must do twice as well as men to be thought half as good. Luckily, this is not difficult.
Charlotte Whitton

A woman can say more in a sigh than a man can say in a sermon.
Arnold Haultain

I took my husband to the hospital yesterday to have 17 stitches out. That'll teach him to buy me a sewing kit for my birthday.
Jo Brand

Careful grooming may take twenty years off a woman's age, but you can't fool a flight of stairs.
Marlene Dietrich

I would rather trust a woman's instinct than a man's reason.
Stanley Baldwin

There are only three things women need in life: food, water, and compliments.
Chris Rock

Compliments cost nothing, and so they are of little value to any except fools and women.
Spandrell

The average woman would rather have beauty than brains, because the average man can see better than he can think.
Anon

Women have a wonderful instinct about things. They can discover everything except the obvious.
Oscar Wilde

A pessimist is a man who thinks all women are bad. An optimist is a man who hopes they are.
Chauncey Mitchell Depew

If it can't be fixed by duct tape or WD-40, it's a female problem.
Jason Love

There's a difference between beauty and charm. A beautiful woman is one I notice. A charming woman is one who notices me.
John Erskine

Well-behaved women rarely make history.
Laurel Thatcher Ulrich

She's the kind of girl who climbed the ladder of success wrong by wrong.
Mae West

She was what we used to call a suicide blond — dyed by her own hand.
Saul Bellow

The only good thing about going bra-less at my age is that it pulls the wrinkles right out of my face.

Anon

CHAPTER 40: WORK

I want to share something with you: The three little sentences that will get you through life:
Number 1: Cover for me.
Number 2: Oh, good idea, Boss!
Number 3: It was like that when I got here.
Homer Simpson

If hard work were such a wonderful thing, surely the rich would have kept it all to themselves.
Lane Kirkland

No man goes before his time - unless the boss leaves early.
Groucho Marx

Hard work is damn near as overrated as monogamy.
Huey P. Long

I will always choose a lazy person to do a hard job, because a lazy person will find an easy way to do it.
Bill Gates

I like work: it fascinates me. I can sit and look at it for hours.
Jerome K. Jerome

Nothing is really work unless you would rather be doing something else.
J.M. Barrie

The caterpillar does all the work, but the butterfly gets all the publicity.
George Carlin

A dog that barks much is never a good hunter.
Proverb

Work is accomplished by those employees who have not yet reached their level of incompetence.
Dr. Laurence J. Peter

It's a recession when your neighbor loses his job; it's a depression when you lose your own.
Harry Truman

The person with the best job in the country is the vice president. All he has to do is get up every morning and say, "How is the president?"
Will Rogers

A consultant is a man who knows 157 ways to make love, but doesn't know any women.
Anon

Experience is what you get when you don't get what you want.
Tori Filler

Work is a refuge of people who have nothing better to do.
Oscar Wilde

The world is full of willing people, some willing to work, the rest willing to let them.
Robert Frost

The best way to appreciate your job is to imagine yourself without one.
Oscar Wilde

Good judgment comes from experience, and experience comes from bad judgment.
Rita Mae Brown

You can't build a reputation on what you are going to do.
Henry Ford

No one's dream job involves a kiosk.
Damien Fahey

Doing nothing is very hard to do...you never know when you're finished.
Leslie Nielsen

An expert is a man who tells you a simple thing in a confused way in such a fashion as to make you think the confusion is your own fault.
William Castle

Hear no evil, see no evil, and speak no evil -- and you'll never get a job working for a tabloid.
Phil Pastoret

ONE LAST THING...

If you enjoyed this book or found it useful I'd be very grateful if you'd post a short review on Amazon. Your support really does make a difference and I read all the reviews personally so I can get your feedback and make this book even better.

If you'd like to leave a review, then all you need to do is click the review link on this book's page on Amazon.

Thank you.

Made in the USA
Middletown, DE
10 December 2020